AUSTIN-HEALEY

Graham Robson

SHIRE PUBLICATIONS

Published in Great Britain in 2010 by Shire Publications Ltd, Midland House, West Way, Botley, Oxford OX2 0PH, United Kingdom.

44-02 23rd Street, Suite 219, Long Island City, NY 11101, USA.

E-mail: shire@shirebooks.co.uk   www.shirebooks.co.uk

A CIP catalogue record for this book is available from the British Library.

Shire Library no. 585   •   ISBN-13: 978 0 74780 769 8

Graham Robson has asserted his right under the Copyright, Designs and Patents Act, 1988, to be identified as the author of this book.

Designed by Ken Vail Graphic Design, Cambridge, UK and typeset in Perpetua and Gill Sans.
Printed in China through Worldprint Ltd.

10 11 12 13 14   10 9 8 7 6 5 4 3 2 1

COVER IMAGE
The original Austin-Healey 100 went on sale in 1953, with a sleek style that needed no change for the next two decades. With a top speed of nearly 105 mph, this was a very popular sports car.

TITLE PAGE IMAGE
Famous badge, famous car: the legendary Austin-Healey marque was created in 1952 with a famous handshake deal between Donald Healey and BMC chairman Leonard Lord.

CONTENTS PAGE IMAGE
As advertised in the early 1960s, the Healey 3000 was claimed to be 'way ahead for pace and reliability, it offers safe, sports car motoring for the family – You can depend on it.'

ACKNOWLEDGEMENTS
I could never have written any of my Austin-Healey books without a great deal of help and support from the Healey family itself – most notably Donald Healey, Geoffrey Healey, Margot Healey, and Brian ('Bic') Healey.

Bill Piggott, a distinguished Austin-Healey historian, has provided the majority of the images used in this book, notably some of the very rare BMC adverts which add a wonderfully nostalgic flavour to the story.

Previously, when he was at the British Motor Industry Heritage Trust, Anders Clausager provided much valuable information about production and factory locations.

Bill and I also thank the following for providing images: John Bowman, Peter Browning, Mirco Decet, Bob Kemp, Georg Sander (page 62), and Alan Twitchett.

Graham Robson

CONTENTS

ANCESTORS AND 'WARWICK HEALEYS'

THE AUSTIN-HEALEY story centred on just two people: Donald Healey, who founded the Healey company, and Sir Leonard Lord, who was chairman of the British Motor Corporation (BMC) in the 1940s and 1950s. BMC, then Britain's largest car-maker, whose brands included the mass-market Austin, had the factories, the financial backing and the industrial muscle. Healey had the technical nous, a flair for design and styling, and the ambition to build sports cars, while Lord had the drive and desire to add a new brand to BMC's portfolio.

When Healey and Lord finally got together in 1952, both had already been in the British motor industry for three decades. Leonard Lord, born in Coventry in 1896, had been apprenticed to Courtaulds and then joined the engine-builders Hotchkiss (which became Morris Engines), before becoming a much-respected production engineer and manager first at Wolseley, then at Morris Motors. Having become managing director at Morris, he transformed that business but quarrelled with its founder, Lord Nuffield, and stormed out. Later, he joined Austin in 1938 and became that company's chairman in 1945. It was at his suggestion that Austin merged with the Nuffield Organisation in 1952 to form BMC, after which he was literally 'Lord' of all he surveyed.

Donald Mitchell Healey was born in 1898 in Perranporth, Cornwall, where his family ran the local general store. Having been apprenticed to the Sopwith Aviation Company in Kingston-upon-Thames, Surrey, DMH (as he was invariably known), joined the Royal Flying Corps during the First World War. After crashing several times, he was invalided out, and after the war he opened a garage business in Perranporth.

This was where the connection between Healey and fast motor cars was founded. Not only did DMH drive the best and most sporting of what we now know as 'vintage' cars in the 1920s, but he became a noted and successful competition driver. In later years, although he was not a formally trained engineer and designer, he always had very firm ideas of what he wanted and could inspire entire teams to do his bidding. From 1930 he began driving factory-loaned Invicta cars and won the Monte Carlo Rally in a 4.5-litre example in 1931. From 1933 he was persuaded to move to Coventry, where he originally joined Riley as a development engineer (the Imp and MPH sports cars came along at this time), but he soon moved across the city to Triumph, where he quickly became technical director and oversaw the design of the noted Gloria, Vitesse and Dolomite ranges. One intriguing 'super-car' project, the Dolomite Straight Eight, was abandoned before it reached production.

Times were hard for small car-making companies in the late 1930s, so when Triumph's finances collapsed in 1939 Healey soon moved to Humber Ltd (the major arm of the burgeoning Rootes Group) and spent the Second World War designing and proving military vehicles. Although his ambition was to return to Triumph and ease that company back into the car-making business, he could not do it on his own terms (and Triumph was eventually absorbed by Standard).

It was at this time that his thoughts first turned to making a 'Healey' sports car, though investment capital was always going to be a problem. Originally he considered using Triumph running gear, but he finally settled on Riley engines and transmissions. By 1946, with much of the chassis designed by a team that included his son Geoffrey, he was able to launch the first ever Healey sports car.

Donald Healey: visionary, publicist, businessman, competition driver – and inventor of the Healey and Austin-Healey brands. His life in motoring stretched from the 1920s to the 1970s.

In 1946 Donald Healey launched his own brand of car from a factory in Warwick. This was the Elliot two-door saloon, with Riley engines, and much larger and more expensive than the 100/4 would be. The original 'Warwick Healeys' of the late 1940s used this type of front grille, which was adapted, in wider, flatter, but still distinct form, for the 100/4 of 1953.

Until the Austin-Healey 100 was born, the 100 bhp Riley-engined Healey Silverstone was the fiercest two-seater being built at Warwick.

These cars were built in small ramshackle premises on an industrial estate in Warwick, just south of Coventry, and so the cars became known among enthusiasts as 'Warwick Healeys'. For the next six years – until the original Austin-Healey came along – every 'Warwick Healey' was based on the same chassis, which incorporated trailing link independent front suspension.

Because Healey was always a small and under-capitalised concern, whose cars were relatively costly, annual sales were measured in hundreds, rather

The very first 'Healey 100' was completed in the autumn of 1952 and looked less graceful than the production-ready car would. This first machine (which is carrying a false registration number) had disc road wheels, a distinctly 'rough and ready' soft top, and a rather prominent exhaust pipe.

than thousands. For the same reason, there was no way that it could build its own bodies, these therefore being provided by concerns as diverse as Westland, Abbott, Elliott and Tickford. A stark two-seater called the Silverstone and the Nash-Healey (with an engine from the American concern) provided variety in this very popular line-up.

By 1951–2, however, Donald Healey concluded that he needed to start developing a cheaper and simpler model, so that the marque could appeal to more and more enthusiasts. But it was never going to be easy. To develop a smaller, faster and more nimble two-seater

model, he would have to start again, with a new chassis layout, a new engine/transmission package and a single new body style. This was the point at which the car we now know as the Austin-Healey 100 was born, though it was originally called a Healey 100. It would be the first of an illustrious line and would found a dynasty of cars that would continue for almost thirty years and become famous all over the world.

Donald Healey and driver John Sprinzel blowing out an Austin-Healey twenty-fifth anniversary cake in 1977, with Donald's son Geoffrey in the background. They all played important parts in the birth and development of the original Austin-Healey brand.

Four important characters in the Austin-Healey story: (from left to right) Donald Healey, George Harriman (of BMC), Leonard Lord and Lord Nuffield.

BEAUTIFULLY FAST,
THE AUSTIN HEALEY

Shirt and Accessories by Woollands of Knightsbridge

This is an unusual picture. It shows an Austin Healey at rest; and that is one thing this magnificent sports car rarely is. For when you think of an Austin Healey, you think of beauty in action. You think of an immensely powerful sports car going ahead like streak lightning. You think of a speedometer that goes 70 . . . 80 . . . 90 . . . 100 – and more. You think of the sheer excitement and exhilaration of being at the wheel of a record-breaker.

But the Austin Healey is not only beautiful to watch and beautiful to drive. The car itself is a beautiful engineering and design job. Its surging power comes from a superb 2.6 litre O.H.V. engine. Its wonderfully finished body is built on aerodynamic lines for speed. Its controls (one of the results of racing experience) are handily placed for sports driving. Its boot is particularly large for this kind of car. One final word. The upholstery is real leather, the carpeting is luxurious, the accessories are part and parcel of the standard equipment. Considering all this and the class of the car, the price of the Austin Healey is remarkably reasonable: £806 plus £404. 7s. P.T.

AUSTIN HEALE

The Austin Motor Company Limited, Longbridge, Birmingham

AUSTIN AND HEALEY:
THE GRAND ALLIANCE

THE ORIGINAL Healey 100 of 1952 was an amalgam of inspiration by Donald Healey, engineering by a small team led by his son Geoffrey, and body style by Gerry Coker (with input from the coachbuilders Tickford). Because the team was so small, and the size and financial capabilities of the Healey company were so modest, the layout was kept simple, with a front engine, rear-wheel drive and a rugged steel platform to which much of the inner body structure would be welded on assembly. The style was instantly recognisable, featured removable side screens in the doors, and had a windscreen that could be folded flat if weather conditions encouraged it. Because of the panel profiles, the luggage space was quite restricted, but few seemed to care about that.

Donald Healey knew that he could not afford to develop unique running gear of any type, so he decided to source all major components – engines, transmissions, front suspension and steering gear – from BMC at Longbridge, these mainly being lightly modified versions of those already in use in the Austin A90 Atlantic. BMC components were used so widely, and in so diverse a range, that the Healey running gear had close relatives in the A70 Hereford, and in the Austin taxicabs that dominated the market in London and other cities.

Although the sports car that went on sale in 1953 as the Austin-Healey 100 looked the same as the Healey 100 prototype of 1952, the simple addition of 'Austin' to the brand name made all the difference to the car's prospects. When the original car was being developed at Warwick, the idea was to take underframes from John Thompson Motor Pressings of Wolverhampton, body shells from Tickford of Newport Pagnell, and all the running gear from BMC at Longbridge, but to assemble the cars at Warwick. Because the Warwick premises were so small, no more than about ten cars could have been completed every week, and the original pre-tax selling price would have been set at £850.

On completion, the first prototype was given a blast up and down the Jabbeke motor road in Belgium (where it attained 111 mph and made many

Opposite:
The model in this shot of a BN2 is wearing clothes by Woollands of Knightsbridge, in London. The message is clear.

A fun run for 'Big Healeys', with a 100/4 leading a 3000 in the British sunshine. The Austin-Healey club scene has always been vibrant.

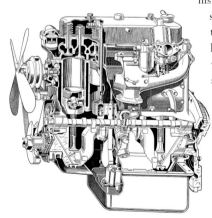

As originally used by Austin in A70 and A90 family cars, this four-cylinder engine had no sporting pretensions. Healey, however, adopted it, in 2.7-litre/A90 guise, for the original 100/4, and generations of owners found that it was a rugged and totally suitable source of power.

headlines) and then readied for display at the London Motor Show at Earl's Court in October. On the speed runs it used steel wheels, but for the show it was fitted with centre-lock wire-spoke wheels, which looked much smarter. That first car used a four-speed gearbox, which would soon be abandoned.

Although BMC's chairman, Leonard Lord, knew of the project in advance, it was his viewing of the prototype at Earl's Court that inspired his offer to take over assembly, distribution and marketing of the car. That, and his instant decision to reduce the selling price to a mere £750, and to lay down capacity to build one hundred or more cars every week, did much to ensure its success in early years. In the United States the original price was held to $3,000.

Under the new deal, Healey would complete the development of the new car (which included slightly restyling the nose, increasing the size of the drum brakes,

Geoffrey Healey with his wife, Margot, in a very early 1953 BN1 – a car still owned and cherished by John Wheatley, who bought it when it was new.

MWD 360 is thought to be the very first 'production-standard' 100/4 of 1953, though even at this stage the headlamps had still to be raised, and the grille still had the distinct peak, which would shortly disappear.

and rearranging the gearbox to provide three forward speeds plus overdrive on top and second gears, instead of the four speeds but no overdrive of the prototype), while BMC would arrange for series production to start as soon as possible.

BMC chairman Leonard Lord wishing good luck to Donald Healey before the latter set off in a prototype 100/4 on its very first sales tour of North America in early 1953.

Complete, partly trimmed Austin-Healey body shells were transported from Jensen in West Bromwich to the final assembly plant (originally Longbridge) in specially developed BMC transporters such as this.

Assembly of the Healey 100/4 would always be a complex business. Underframes came from John Thompson Motor Pressings at Wolverhampton, and body pressings from Boulton Paul, while body/chassis assembly and painting were carried out at Jensen Motors in West Bromwich. Engines and transmissions were manufactured at BMC's sprawling factory at Longbridge, in the south-western outskirts of Birmingham, and final assembly was carried out in a corner of that huge complex.

Series production of the BN1, as the model was always known internally, began, on quite a small scale, in the early summer of 1953. Now that BMC's cumbersome purchase, manufacturing and marketing networks had to be considered, they cancelled out the brisk efficiency of the Healey operation,

This cutaway drawing of the original Healey 100 (it was completed before the name change took place) tells us everything about the layout of the new car – showing that the main chassis rails ran underneath the line of the rear axle. The prototype ran on steel disc wheels, but all early production cars had centre lock wires.

though Healey did, at least, build at Warwick the first twenty of what would these days be called 'pilot build' examples: the first cars were shipped to the United States in March 1953. Thereafter, though, only the Special Test Cars, the 100M (see below) and the 100S, would be constructed in the Warwick workshops.

Assembly of four-cylinder Austin-Healeys was located in a dedicated corner of BMC's sprawling factory at Longbridge. This early shot, taken on 28 September 1953, shows the Jensen-built body/chassis units being united with Austin engines and transmissions.

Specially shot for a tuning manual concerning these cars, this photograph shows an early BN1 at high speed on the banked track at the MIRA proving ground, near Nuneaton. On a later occasion, BMC cheated by flipping the negative to show a supposedly left-hand-drive car circulating in the other direction, but few people were fooled.

Over the next four years the 100/4's reputation as a fine new brand of sports car was first laid, later established, and soon confirmed. Like rival cars such as the MG MGA and the Triumph TR2, it was primarily intended to appeal to customers in North America, who flocked to it in great numbers. In four years the styling did not alter in any way, though the specification gradually settled down, and the reputation grew. Starting at Longbridge

The 100/4 went on sale in 1953, with this simple but neatly laid-out fascia panel. Comfortable, but strictly two-seater, this was always a low-slung sports car.

The fold-flat windscreen was one of the most ingenious and well-liked features of the original Austin-Healey 100. When the weather was favourable, it was an extremely pleasant way of driving this sports car.

BEAUTIFULLY FAST,
THE AUSTIN HEALEY

Mohair Coat & Jersey Hat by Jaeger

This is an unusual picture. It shows an Austin Healey at rest; and that is one thing this magnificent sports car rarely is. For when you think of an Austin Healey, you think of beauty in action. You think of an immensely powerful sports car going ahead like streak lightning. You think of a speedometer that goes 70 ... 80 ... 90 ... 100 — and more. You think of the sheer excitement and exhilaration of being at the wheel of a record-breaker.

But the Austin Healey is not only beautiful to watch and beautiful to drive. The car itself is a beautiful engineering and design job. Its surging power comes from a superb 2.6 litre O.H.V. engine. Its wonderfully finished body is built on aerodynamic lines for speed. Its controls (one of the results of racing experience) are handily placed for sports driving. Its boot is particularly large for this kind of car. One final word. The upholstery is real leather, the carpeting is luxurious, the accessories are part and parcel of the standard equipment. Considering all this and the class of the car, the price of the Austin Healey is remarkably reasonable.

Austin of England

Austin Motor Export Corporation Limited, Birmingham, England

BMC often aimed its Austin-Healey advertising at wealthier customers, this four-cylinder car being graced by a very elegant model, a toy big cat, and a note that the clothing came from Jaeger.

in May 1953, 1,274 cars were produced in the first year, followed by 5,940 cars in 1954, by which time the production line was already flowing at top speed. It did not flag – not even when those assembly lines were moved to the MG plant at Abingdon in 1957 – for another fifteen years.

Very early cars incorporated some aluminium skin panels (the 1953 models, therefore, were the lightest types of all), but by mid-1954 the 100/4 was an all-steel machine and would remain so thereafter. At the same time, more and more performance-enhancing options were made available.

Healey assembled fifteen identical BN2s for use in a Formula 1 drivers' parade at the British Grand Prix at Aintree in July 1955.

The big change followed in the autumn of 1955, when the 100/4 (which continued to use components from the latest, newly launched BMC saloon cars) became the BN2 type; this featured a new type of four-speed (instead of three-speed) gearbox which was being fitted to the Austin A90 Westminster saloon: overdrive was still standard. This car was eventually replaced by the first of the six-cylinder Austin-Healeys – the 100-Six – in 1956.

Donald Healey himself ran this specially built 100/4, complete with a permanent hardtop, during the 1950s.

Model Angela Lane posed with this 1955 100M BN2 at the Saxon Mill Hotel, which was close enough to the Warwick premises to be Healey's 'local'.

100M — 'M' FOR LE MANS

In the last year of 100/4 production, and officially starting from October 1955, when it was announced, the 100M conversion kit was launched, for which British customers paid £105 extra (and Americans $290 extra). In appearance, this involved the fitment of a louvred bonnet panel (the better to extract air from the engine bay), which was held down by a leather bonnet strap, and often (but not always) by the application of dual-tone paintwork.

In 1955 and 1956 a large number of 100/4s were converted to 100M condition, which also included more powerful engines and stiffened-up suspension. In all cases, these cars started life as standard production machines, to which the performance kits were later added. This was directly influenced by the brand's fine performance at the Le Mans 24 Hour Race in 1953, and because of a constant demand for a higher performance derivative. There has always been controversy about the numbers actually built, not because BMC wanted to keep this a secret, but because 100Ms were created in three ways: either by being converted at Longbridge after assembly; by being converted by Healey at Warwick; or by being converted at Austin-Healey dealerships after the standard cars arrived there. Individual totals have often been in dispute, but no less an authority than Geoffrey Healey states that a grand total of 1,159 100Ms were eventually produced. This, of course, was at the time, for it was always possible (and was done) for a 100M to be created at a later date by fitting the appropriate pieces of kit.

The chassis was improved with modified damper settings, and by the use of a stiffer front

When complete with two-tone paintwork, a louvred bonnet and the strap to hold down the bonnet, the 100M was a very attractive car.

Bill Piggott, the noted Austin-Healey historian, and researcher of every image used in this book, enjoys a fun run in his carefully maintained 100/4.

suspension anti-roll bar, but the major change was to the engine, which became the 'P280' type, complete with larger SU carburettors, a different camshaft profile, high compression pistons, different valve gear and other details – and produced no less than 110 bhp at 4,500 rpm. The top speed was 109 mph, making this the best all-round 100/4 type – though the 100S (described below) was faster, but less civilised.

100S – A RACING DIVERSION

Because there was a demand for high-performance derivatives of the 100/4, and because Healey was still enthusiastic about motor racing, BMC allowed them to develop a special version at Warwick, and to sell it from there. This machine, built in tiny quantities (there would be just fifty 'production' types) was the 100S, which was the ultimate in four-cylinder Austin-Healeys.

Inspired by Healey's own 'Special Test Cars' (the race and record-attempt machines are described more fully in the chapter on motor sport), the 100S was lighter where possible, with much more powerful engines and far better brakes. For all that, it was a practical road car too, if far from refined.

Compared with the 100/4, the 100S (the 'S' stood for Sebring, the famous racing circuit in Florida) looked very similar, though it had a rounded radiator grille, and there was no provision for bumpers, full-size windscreen, side curtains or even a hood. Luggage space was even more restricted than usual, for there was a massive 20-gallon fuel tank in the tail. The entire body skin was made from light-alloy (instead of steel) panels, and looked purposeful and wind-cheating.

Under the skin the 100S featured a strengthened chassis frame, with provision for larger Armstrong rear dampers, and was fitted with four-wheel Dunlop disc brakes (the 100/4 still used drums), but the major changes were to engine and transmission. Not only did the 100S have a four-speed gearbox

Brian ('Bic') Healey, Donald Healey's youngest son, at the wheel of a 100S production car, outside the experimental department at the Healey factory in Warwick.

THE *Austin Healey* 100 S

Built for Racing — by Racing Specialists

Above: Although the colour wash is in a rather bilious green, this study shows the unmistakable style of the 100S, which was revealed at the Earl's Court Motor Show of 1954. 'Built for Racing' tells its own story, for this machine had aluminium bodywork and a 132 bhp engine.

CSJ 725

A restored 100S photographed in a typically peaceful English village.

The 100S, intended for motor racing, but also a super-fast road car, was introduced in 1954. A total of only fifty-five cars was maufactured before production ended in 1955 (five of these being 'Special Test Cars' owned by the Healey family). Most of the cars survive to this day.

(but no overdrive), but the 2,660cc engine had been completely reworked, now having a new light-alloy cylinder head by Weslake, which helped to produce a full 132 bhp, with a commensurate increase in mid-range torque.

Never actively marketed in the United Kingdom (only six cars were originally allocated to British customers), the 100S was aimed at North America and other export markets. All fifty cars were assembled at Warwick in 1955 (since 'Warwick Healey' assembly had recently ended, there was space in the aging buildings), and when that production run was completed the model was quietly discontinued. Like many such ultra-special models, demand was always going to be low, but the impact the 100S had on the brand's reputation was considerable.

AUSTIN-HEALEY 100/4

Specifications:

2,660cc four-cylinder engine. 90 bhp (100/4), 110 bhp (100M) or 132 bhp (100S).

Three-speed plus overdrive, or four-speed plus overdrive (100/4), or four-speed (100S).

Wheelbase:

7 feet 6 inches.

Unladen weight:

2,015 pounds (original 100/4), or 1,924 pounds (100S).

Top speed:

103 mph (100/4) or 125 mph (100S).

Production:

14,634 (100/4), 50 (100S).

Left: No sooner had the 100/4 gone on sale than the first colour advertisements appeared. This shot is thought to have been taken at Llandrindod Wells in central Wales.

Below: A gentlemanly way of selling sports cars: this BMC showroom, thought to be in London, seems quiet, calm, and not at all linked to sports-car motoring. Note the Austin J40 toy cars.

100-SIX AND 3000:
THE CLASSIC 'BIG HEALEY'

AUSTIN-HEALEY underwent major changes between 1956 and 1958. Not only did the original 100/4 give way to a much-modified six-cylinder car (the 100-Six), but assembly of those cars was then moved south to the MG factory at Abingdon, Oxfordshire. Within a year the relocated 100-Six lines were joined by a cute small Austin-Healey, the later famous 'Frog-eye' Sprite. Thenceforward, Abingdon became BMC's dedicated sports-car factory, with Austin-Healey and MG sharing the site.

Given how BMC's production facilities were changing in the mid-1950s, modifications to the 100/4 became inevitable – though few expected a new model to be quite so different from the original. With the 100/4's four-cylinder engine all but obsolete by 1956, perhaps it was logical to expect a new six-cylinder power-unit to be adopted – but surely not in a longer, heavier and somehow less pure version of the original.

Without doubt the new model was an Austin-Healey with many BMC ideas imposed on the Healey engineers at Warwick, who hated to see weight and bulk being added to any of their cars. This was the first model to be known by the sobriquet 'Big Healey', which gradually became a term of real endearment.

Launched in August 1956, the 100-Six (known internally as BN4) featured a modified 100/4 structure in which the wheelbase had been stretched by 2 inches, with tiny 'plus-two' seating inserted behind the front seats. An 'Austin-type' radiator grille mesh was adopted and a bonnet scoop was included to clear the rather bulky six-cylinder engine, and the resulting front-end style changes were not universally liked. These covered a new-generation 2.6-litre six-cylinder engine – the BMC C-Series type, which was intended for use in many future models and light commercial vehicles. Although this was more powerful (102 bhp, as opposed to 90 bhp) than the obsolete 2.6-litre 'Four', it was also heavier than before and originally had a not very efficient type of cast-iron cylinder head.

Furthermore, BMC's cost controllers, and the marketing staff, had stripped out the specification, compared to the 100/4. Pressed-steel rather

Opposite:
After Austin-Healey assembly was moved from Longbridge to Abingdon in 1957, the cars were built alongside MG sports cars. 'Frog-eye' Sprite assembly also took place here.

When the 100-Six was introduced in 1956, it had disc wheels as standard equipment, in contrast to the wire-spoke wheels on the earlier 100/4.

than wire-spoke wheels had become standard (the wires were now to be optional extras), while overdrive and even the heater became extras. The new type, too, was available with a smart removable hardtop, but examples were surprisingly rare, even after becoming famous on the 'works' competition cars.

In the 1950s BMC was wedded to an image of motoring that featured a sports car, peaked cap, moustache and country casual clothing. This is how the first six-cylinder 100-Six was launched in 1956, showing off the bulk of the six-cylinder engine.

UOC 741 started life as a 100-Six used for sedate publicity shots in 1956 (though note the Dunlop racing tyres), went on to be used for motor-sport development by Healey at Warwick, and finally became a full-blooded factory rally car in 1958.

Intended, as ever, to appeal to the export market rather than domestic buyers, the new 100-Six offered a bit more space, a little more versatility, and a longer list of options without what Americans called the 'sticker price' being affected too much, and at least it was available in big numbers well before the end of 1956. There was, however, a problem, for the new type was nearly 300 pounds heavier than the old (and more nose-heavy than before), and the new engine was smooth, but reluctant to rev, so that despite the increase in power output the 100-Six's overall performance was much as before. Press reviews were lukewarm, and urgent changes were required.

Although the optional hardtop was a very smart fitting for 100-Six and 3000 types, it seemed to be surprisingly rare. Even its universal use on factory competition cars did not give it much of a boost.

Personalities sold cars in the 1950s, as they still do today. In 1958, when the latest 117 bhp engine was introduced in the 100-Six, BMC used the top racing driver Roy Salvadori and the BBC motor-racing commentator (and *Autosport* columnist) John Bolster to sing its praises.

'an impressive increase in punch'

John Bolster and Roy Salvadori put the latest Austin Healey 100 Six through its paces.

BOLSTER How do you find her with the new cylinder head, Roy?

SALVADORI This new 6-port induction system gives her an impressive increase in punch, particularly in top from 50 to 80. You know the technical story — one port to each cylinder means vastly better gas flow. The upshot of it is, BHP is now 117 at 4,750 revs. The Austin Healey always had plenty of dig, but now it's really outstanding.

BOLSTER Does her handling match up to this performance?

SALVADORI Oh, more than that. Push her really hard (she's a first-rate sprint car) and she still handles beautifully. The gear-change is as slick as they come, and the ratios are just the job for fast work on the intermediates.

BOLSTER How about finish? Not exactly Spartan, is she?

SALVADORI No, thank goodness. I sell Austin Healeys and I know my customers. Sleek lines, modern colour schemes, leather upholstery, the lot — that's what they want and that's what they get. This car's a gem.

BOLSTER Speaking as a racing driver or a salesman, Roy?

SALVADORI Both, old boy.

AUSTIN HEALEY

THE AUSTIN MOTOR COMPANY LIMITED · LONGBRIDGE · BIRMINGHAM

To its credit, BMC acknowledged this within months and set about a series of updates, which somehow became entangled with the move of final assembly to the MG plant at Abingdon. First of all came the launch of a much-improved cylinder head for the engine, which revved more freely and produced 117 bhp. This was soon followed up with the BN6 type, which was a reversion to the 'classic' two-seater cockpit style of the 100/4. BN4 and BN6 types were thereafter available side by side, though the demand for two-seater types gradually fell away.

When *The Motor* published a special 'Sports Car Number' in 1958, BMC placed an advertisement for the latest 100-Six on the front cover.

In the same period, and to the lasting confusion of statisticians and historians, although the BN4 assembly facility was moved from Longbridge to the MG factory at Abingdon before the end of 1957, BN6 assembly did not start up until the Abingdon move had been completed. As ever, manufacture of body/chassis assemblies stayed at Jensen, which meant that delivery (by truck) to Abingdon was considerably lengthier than before. Luckily, this was achieved without any overall loss of production or sales, for the body/chassis assembly process at Jensen was always very efficient.

In 1958 the Cambridge University Automobile Club borrowed a 100-Six from the factory, had it specially prepared, and used it to break a succession of endurance records on the Montlhéry banked track in France.

With 117 bhp types now capable of 111 mph, and with much of the original sporting character restored to the package, the clientele was happy with the latest cars, of which more than seven thousand were being sold in some calendar years. A big majority of all these went to export territories. The next big change followed in the summer of 1959, when, with all Austin-Healey assembly now centred at Abingdon, the 100-Six gave way to a car called the 3000. Although there were no style changes, and this car was still available in two-seater or notional two-plus-two form, this time it had a 124 bhp/2,912cc version of the engine and was fitted with disc front brakes. To complete the transformation, a new model logo – '3000' in this case – was affixed to the car's front grille.

Thus the 'Big Healey', as everyone now seemed to nickname it, started a career that was to last for nearly nine years, with several major changes and improvements being introduced during that period. A production car that would finally be made obsolete only by the onset of new safety and engine exhaust emission regulations in the United States, which effectively outlawed it, the 3000 was also the basis of a formidably successful race and rally car, as described in a later chapter.

In all that time there was only one important style change – when the Mark II Sports Convertible appeared in 1962 – though the brawny six-cylinder engine became progressively more powerful, and vehicle performance increased to match it, while one important chassis improvement was phased in during 1964. This was the period in which there were two highly successful Austin-Healeys on the market, Sprite and 3000 – which made the marque at least as important to BMC's image as the MGs built alongside them – and when the Healey family was not only well favoured by management, but encouraged to start thinking about the future. Unhappily, as we now know, this co-operation was finally cast to the winds

Austin Healey 3000

2-seater and occasional 4-seater sports cars

When the 3000 was introduced in 1959, BMC was clearly still aiming at the middle-class market, where it thought the Austin-Healey brand belonged.

Introduced on the 100-Six in 1956, the BMC C-Series engine eventually grew to 2.9 litres and a torquey 148 bhp for the 3000 Mark III.

when BMC was absorbed into the new British Leyland organisation in 1968.

Early in the 1960s Healey, and their new-found colleagues at Abingdon, brought forward a series of developments to the 'Big Healey' pedigree, with every change seeming to improve, if only in detail, on what had gone before. Sales held up remarkably well as year followed year without a styling change – 7,005 were built in 1960, 4,663 in 1962 and 4,874 in 1964, for instance – this certainly being sustained by constant praise in the specialist press, and by a run of great sporting success in rallies and on the race tracks of the world.

An unlikely story, but true: Peter Browning, on his way to run the timing of the BMC race effort at Le Mans, France, in 1964, towed this caravan all the way behind a Mark III. Unhappily the car was never intended to do this, so progress was very slow.

Assembly of 3000 Mark III body/chassis units at Jensen in the mid-1960s. Jensen held this build contract from 1953 to the end of the line in 1967.

Imperceptibly but definitely, though, the sturdy 'Old English' character of the model began to dominate all discussion about the car. Because of the rorty, sometimes noisy nature of the engine, and the rather unforgiving ride qualities, the 'Big Healey' was often described as 'traditional', a 'he-man's car' or 'hairy-chested', reflecting the fact that the cars were simply engineered, traded fresh-air enjoyment for refinement and did not have such chi-chi features as power-assisted steering or soft and pliant suspension.

What they did have, unquestionably, was power and torque, and those characteristics improved as time passed. From 1961 the original 3000 gave way to the Mark II, in which the engine got three SU carburettors (instead of two) and 132 bhp, but this was soon followed by a major re-engineering

From the summer of 1962, the 'Big Healey' officially became the Mark IIA Sports Convertible, with wind-up windows in the doors, and a larger, fixed, wrap-around windscreen.

Even after fifteen years, the 'Big Healey' shape still looked handsome. This was a 1966-built example, of the type known to all Healey enthusiasts as a 'BJ8'.

of the centre body shell in the summer of 1962, when a car rather clumsily known as the '3000 Mark II Sports Convertible' arrived.

This was a real advance – the first, really, since 1952 – for the doors had been redesigned to accommodate wind-up drop-glass windows, the windscreen was reshaped to be larger and wrap-around, and there was a new fold-away soft top. The result was a more modern-feeling car, a little heavier than before, but competitive both in looks and behaviour. The fact that the engine had reverted to twin SU carburettors (and a slight loss of peak power, to 131 bhp) was not considered important. *Autocar* testers commented on 'the first real move to increase the refinement and convenience of the car as a whole, widening its appeal...'.

There was still more to come, however, for in the spring of 1964 the final derivative, the Mark III, appeared, benefiting from a reworked cabin, with better seats and a central oddments box in the centre console, a redesigned wooden-faced instrument panel, and a versatile 'plus-two' seating area, which incorporated a fold-down parcel shelf. Also, the engine was again retuned, now producing a very brawny 148 bhp, and endowing the car with a top speed of more than 120 mph.

The first 1,390 of this derivative used the same rear suspension as before, but after that there was a final change: the steel chassis rails (which ran underneath the line of the rear axle) were profiled to allow more movement, twin trailing radius arms were added, and the traditional Panhard rod was finally abandoned. Such changes had already been blooded in motor sport and had proved that the softer-sprung car had better track and handling balance.

Although the little Sprite, described separately, was now selling in considerably higher numbers than the 3000, the larger car carried on steadily

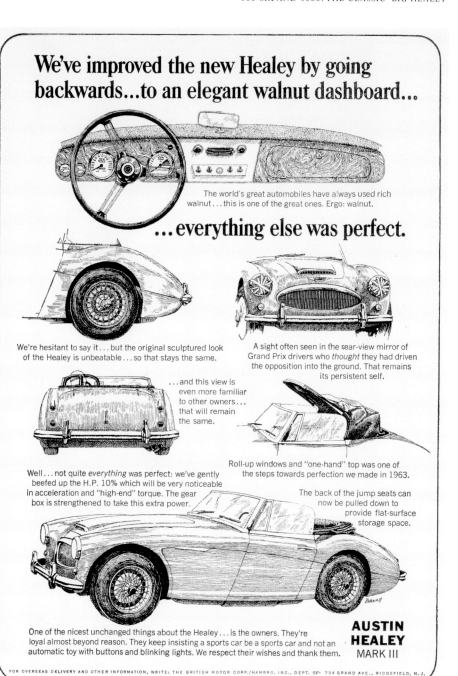

We've improved the new Healey by going backwards...to an elegant walnut dashboard...

The world's great automobiles have always used rich walnut...this is one of the great ones. Ergo: walnut.

...everything else was perfect.

We're hesitant to say it...but the original sculptured look of the Healey is unbeatable...so that stays the same.

A sight often seen in the rear-view mirror of Grand Prix drivers who *thought* they had driven the opposition into the ground. That remains its persistent self.

...and this view is even more familiar to other owners... that will remain the same.

Roll-up windows and "one-hand" top was one of the steps towards perfection we made in 1963.

Well...not quite *everything* was perfect: we've gently beefed up the H.P. 10% which will be very noticeable in acceleration and "high-end" torque. The gear box is strengthened to take this extra power.

The back of the jump seats can now be pulled down to provide flat-surface storage space.

One of the nicest unchanged things about the Healey...is the owners. They're loyal almost beyond reason. They keep insisting a sports car be a sports car and not an automatic toy with buttons and blinking lights. We respect their wishes and thank them.

AUSTIN HEALEY
MARK III

FOR OVERSEAS DELIVERY AND OTHER INFORMATION, WRITE: THE BRITISH MOTOR CORP./HAMBRO, INC., DEPT. SF· 734 GRAND AVE., RIDGEFIELD, N.J.

This advertisement shows off the important changes made to the interior of the 3000 Mark III.

until 1967, when a series of proposed regulations concerning crash testing and the limitation of engine exhaust emissions loomed up in North America. The existing 'Big Healey' could not be modified (nor did BMC find it cost-effective to try), so a search for a replacement finally began. Healey had already been thinking about their future but could not go ahead without financial backing from the BMC hierarchy.

As an interim model (perhaps even a final derivative of what already existed), Healey proposed an Austin-Healey '4000', a car that would have had a widened version of the existing chassis, structure and body style, along with a 4-litre six-cylinder Rolls-Royce engine of a type currently being used in an existing BMC saloon car (the Vanden Plas Princess R), while BMC's own designers proposed a 'badge-engineered' version of the forthcoming MG MGC sports car, which was itself based on the structure and style of the existing MG MGB.

Neither of these eventually found favour (though two '4000' prototypes were built), and both projects were cancelled. A later proposal, by BMC, for an all-new 'Austin-Healey' sports car to be designed by themselves, and with styling bought in from outside consultants, was apparently so 'awful (it was nicknamed 'Fireball XL5' after a contemporary television puppet show) that the Healey family would have nothing to do with it, and this too was cancelled after much development work had already been completed.

This smart coupé style was the winner of a design competition set up by Pininfarina in 1962 and was eventually built as a one-off on the chassis of an Austin-Healey 3000. BMC even gave thought to putting it into production, but Donald Healey would never back it.

In the end, the conclusion for the 'Big Healey', but not for the Sprite, came suddenly and decisively at the end of 1967 – before, it should be noted, the formation of British Leyland had taken place. No sooner had the new MG MGC gone into production in October 1967 than assembly of the 3000 began to wind down rapidly. Only fifteen such cars were built in December

The only drawback of a sleek style like this, with tail panels sweeping down to the rear bumper, was that luggage space was restricted. This is a 1966 model.

As the 3000 came towards the end of its life, Healey proposed widening the structure, inserting a Rolls-Royce 4-litre engine, and calling it an Austin-Healey 4000. Two prototypes were produced in 1967.

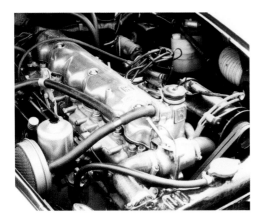

1967, and except for the whimsical building of a single car in March 1968 (to satisfy the strident demands of one particularly vocal enthusiast), they were the last.

Cars of this pedigree, therefore, had been on sale from 1953 to 1968, and more than 73,000 had been produced. Even before the marque had been consigned to history, however, it seemed that a legend was established: one-make preservation clubs sprang up all over the world, and several thousands of these cars were preserved for future enthusiasts to enjoy.

Consider the performance of an Austin-Healey '4000' with a 175 bhp/4-litre Rolls-Royce engine installed. Two prototypes of such a car were built.

One of the very last BJ8s, built in 1967, shows off the low-slung exhaust system for which all these cars were noted.

AUSTIN-HEALEY 100-SIX AND 3000

Specifications:

2,639cc (100-Six) or 2,912cc (3000). 102 bhp or 117 bhp (100-Six), 124 bhp, 131 bhp, 132 bhp or 148 bhp (3000).

Four-speed plus optional overdrive.

Wheelbase:

7 feet 8 inches.

Unladen weight:

2,435 pounds (100-Six) to 2,548 pounds (final 3000).

Top speed:

103 mph (original 100-Six) to 121 mph (final 3000).

Production:

15,444 (100-Six), 42,926 (3000).

Even in 1966, just one year before assembly of the 'Big Healey' ended, the style was almost the same as it had been since the 1950s. The only detail update obvious in this example is the separate side lamp and turn indicators underneath the headlamps.

Healey enthusiasts learned to identify each model by tiny styling changes. In this case, they knew a late-model 3000 by its vertical grille, by the appropriate 'Mk III' badge above it, and by the separate side lamps and turn indicators.

SPRITE: THE SPORTS CAR FOR EVERYONE

ONCE THE Austin-Healey 100/4 had gone into production, BMC's bosses drew the Healey company closer and closer into all its corporate schemes. Not only was the company encouraged to take up various racing and record-breaking activities, but it was consulted about new models.

The demise of one Midget and the eventual introduction of another were both instrumental in the arrival in 1958 of a cute little sports car called the Austin-Healey Sprite. The impetus came from Sir Leonard Lord at BMC but, as with the 100/4, it was still the Healey family who did most of the engineering of the new car.

The story of the Sprite began with the end of the MG TF Midget in 1955 and with Len Lord's recognition of the need for a new entry-level sports car to replace it. (The TF Midget was the last of a long line: it was replaced by the more substantial MGA, a fine sports car, but not in the same size or price class.) In 1956, therefore, Donald Healey was called in and offered the challenge of producing a new two-seater car to be based on the Austin A35 family car's engine, transmission and running gear. It would, he was assured, carry the 'Austin-Healey' identity, though other possibilities might arise in the future. (They did, the MG Midget of 1961 being the result.)

Although he received another assurance – that BMC would cover all development costs and would lay down the facilities to produce cars in big numbers – Healey's challenge was to do the job as quickly as possible. In the event, evolution of the new car progressed from 'good idea' to pilot production in only about eighteen months, which was rapid by contemporary British motor industry standards. With Geoffrey Healey once again leading the engineering team at Warwick, Healey soon produced a simple, short and stubbily styled little two-seater sports car, with removable side screens and a 'build-it-yourself' soft top, after which BMC stepped in to complete development and get the car on sale.

It was not for some time that the new machine gained its 'Sprite' model name, this being a rather complex process. Originally, in the 1930s, Sprites had been Rileys, but by the 1950s that trademark had been acquired by

Opposite:
Brought together to celebrate fifty years of the Sprite, this impressive line at Goodwood features PBL 75, the original 'launch' Sprite, and two well-known Sebring Sprite race cars, including the famous PMO 200 of John Sprinzel.

The packaging of the original Sprite was pure genius, but there was no outside access to the luggage compartment. To reach the spare wheel, one had to go in by way of the passenger compartment.

Daimler, who produced the short-lived Lanchester Sprite, and Sir Leonard Lord needed to apply all his industry muscle to acquire the name for his own cars again.

The new car used a sturdy all-steel monocoque body shell, in which two main features were that the entire front end (nose, bonnet and front wings) was to be built as one and hinged from the bulkhead to the passenger compartment, and that there was to be no external access to the rear stowage

BMC's original Sprite brochure shows off the rather awkward packaging of the original spare wheel, and the way that the entire front end of the bonnet and wings could be lifted up.

PBL 75 was the original Sprite 'publicity car', which appeared in many BMC advertisements and promotional displays of 1958. It survived to celebrate its fiftieth birthday in 2008.

Below left: The original Sprite had a very basic fascia, trim and seating layout. It was strictly a compact two-seater, with removable side curtains for the doors.

area or to the spare wheel. The original intention of using modified Austin A35 running gear throughout was retained as far as possible, except that Healey dumped the A35 steering gear in favour of Morris Minor rack

and pinion, adopted an all-hydraulic braking installation, and laid out a new type of rear suspension where twin trailing quarter-elliptic leaf springs and radius arms supported, located and also sprung the rear axle.

With the 948cc engine initially tuned to produce 43 bhp, a top speed of more than 85 mph was expected, and the only major change that had to be made was that an original proposal to fit 'flip-up' headlamps (a certain minimum height was required to meet British construction and use regulations) was abandoned in favour of mounting fixed headlamps in pods on the bonnet, this ensuring that the new car carried the nickname of 'Frog-eye' (or, in the United States, 'Bug-eye'). Sprites would be 'Frog-eyes' until 1961, after which a restyling made them look much more conventional.

Below: All Sprites were fitted with a derivative of BMC's mass-production A-Series engine. This, the original 948cc unit, shows off the twin-SU carburettors, and the remote-control gear-change mechanism.

The Austin Motor Company has recently made a landmark in motoring history with the announcement of a completely new and inexpensive sports car—the Austin Healey Sprite, powered by a special 948 c.c. A-type engine. It is some 20 years since Austin made a small sports car, but the Sprite lives up fully to the fine tradition established in the 1920's and 30's

BMC was proud of its new baby, this being one of the original press advertisements of 1958.

Although development had been straightforward, getting the car on sale was not. In BMC's master plan, the intention had been to assemble the new Sprite at the vast Austin factory at Longbridge, but that changed when BMC made the strategic decision to concentrate all their sports-car production at the MG plant at Abingdon. The existing six-cylinder Austin-Healey (the 100-Six) was due to make the move before the end of 1957, and the new Sprite was therefore slated to follow in 1958.

The production process confirms how difficult it was, at this time, to make economic sense of the BMC business in general. For the Sprite, chassis platforms were manufactured by John Thompson Motor Pressings in Wolverhampton; body shells were then completed by Pressed Steel at Swindon (which is now a BMW/Mini body facility); painting and part trim were carried out by Pressed Steel at Cowley near Oxford (where Minis are now assembled), before the cars were completed at the MG factory at Abingdon. In the meantime, engines were manufactured by the BMC engines plant in Coventry, with gearboxes and axles coming from BMC factories in Birmingham. Virtually nothing was manufactured, as opposed to screwed

As developed and manufactured by John Sprinzel's London-based tuning company, the alloy-bodied Sebring Sprite was the fiercest of all Sprite derivatives. In the early 1960s it was an excellent car to use on the race track and in rallies.

together, at Abingdon, though all deliveries were made from there. Countless hours were spent in the transfer of pressings, and indeed complete shells, from factory to factory.

Launched in May 1958 and priced at a mere £669 (tax paid), the Sprite was an immediate success, with almost (but not quite) everyone falling for the cute front-end style. The handling and character matched up to the engineering and price. However, a thriving sub-industry rapidly developed in providing restyled front ends made from glass-fibre, so that many Sprites, once crashed, adopted a new and more conventional bonnet in the repair.

Not everyone liked the style of the original 'Frog-eye', so there was a big demand for modified bonnets and hardtops. In 1961 the author's 'Frog-eye' was given an Ashley bonnet like this.

No fewer than 21,566 Sprites were built in the first full year (1959) and, as with the bigger model, most of these cars were sold overseas. Once again Donald Healey's eye for a market opportunity, and for the character of a Healey-badged car, had been proved. It was not long before seemingly every sports-car enthusiast voiced his opinion of how the Sprite might be improved. BMC, for sure, listened closely, the result being a model that was changed frequently, and almost always for the better.

Even as early as 1961, though, BMC diluted the Sprite pedigree. Although they authorised a restyle of the original motor car, they also insisted that a new-generation 'MG Midget' be marketed alongside the revised Sprite,

The Sprite has improved from the inside out

THAT MAKES SENSE

Today's Sprite is the sports car bargain of the world. Its new 1098 c.c. engine sets the pace on the road and the 8¼-in. disc brakes in front justify pace with safety. The Sprite has new details of comfort and smartness—both seats are adjustable; fitted carpets, padded facia, and a new range of colours, all make it a smart car to be in, and to be seen in. At the price of £485 plus £101.12.1 P.T., the Sprite is a sports car that really makes sense!

THE AUSTIN MOTOR COMPANY LTD · LONGBRIDGE · BIRMINGHAM   PERSONAL EXPORTS DIVISION · 41-46 PICCADILLY · LONDON W1

you invest in an **AUSTIN**

An advert proclaims the high quality and value of the Austin-Healey Sprite.

the two cars being utterly identical in all but tiny visual details and different grilles. The 'new shape' Sprite looked much like the forthcoming MG MGB, for it had a conventional front and rear style, complete with a normal separate lift-up bonnet, headlamps mounted on the wings, a squared-up tail section, and a normal boot lid. Engine power went up to 46 bhp, and a gradual upgrade of trim and equipment began.

From this point on, Sprites were built alongside MG Midgets at Abingdon, these being near-identical cars which few could distinguish at a distance. The following table, therefore, is a direct comparison between the types, and an aide-memoire to what they were called:

In the 1960s Sprites (and Midgets) came in many different shapes, which this melée at Thruxton circuit confirms. A Sebring-bodied car tangles with an early 1970s Midget, followed by a specially bonneted Mark I and a 'Frog-eye'.

Year introduced	Austin-Healey model	MG Midget model
1958	Sprite ('Frog-eye')	–
1961	Sprite Mk II	Midget Mk I
1964	Sprite Mk III	Midget Mk II
1966	Sprite Mk IV	Midget Mk III
1970	Last Austin-Healey Sprite built	–
1974	–	Midget 1500
1979	–	Last Midget built

Although there would be many differences – some large, some small – between the Mk II Sprite of 1961 and the last of the line built in 1970 – as the years rolled by the character of this little car never faltered. Each Sprite was a light, compact two-seater, with pin-sharp steering, eager puppy-like handling, and brisk performance, all wrapped around simple running gear and a tiny two-seat cabin.

Although the basic style did not change, regular alterations to details such as grilles, wheels, windscreens, door profiles, fascia layouts and soft-top

By the late 1960s Sprites not only had a 1,275cc engine and wind-up windows in the doors, but a much sleeker folding hood design. Wire-spoke wheels were optional extras.

construction all told the true Sprite enthusiasts which type of car they were looking at. However, if Triumph had not launched their new Spitfire sports car in 1962, which was aiming at the same market sector, there might never have been such a multiplicity of changes, as competition between the types was always intense.

Following the launch of the restyled car called the Mark II (a style, incidentally, which was sometimes scorned at the time because much visual individuality had been lost), the next update came in late 1962, when the engine was boosted to 56 bhp/1,098cc (this long-stroke engine was similar to that used in the then-new BMC 1100 front-wheel-drive saloons), and front disc brakes became standard, though the car was still known as a Mark II.

A further update, in March 1964, was more significant: the rear suspension was revised, this time to have conventional half-elliptic leaf springs; the cockpit was altered, not only with wind-up windows in the doors, but with a deeper windscreen to suit, and a new fascia layout: all matched by a 59 bhp engine with more torque. Thus a quirky-handling car (on-the-limit oversteer could be encouraged with the original type of rear suspension) became more predictable.

Late-model Mark IV Sprites were given a cosmetic make-over – grille, wheels, sills, windscreen surround. This was controversial, to say the least.

More change and improvement followed at the end of 1966, when the Sprite became Mark IV, this being the point at which the definitive shorter-stroke 65 bhp/1,275cc engine was standardised, and the top speed rose to 94 mph. This was a very desirable little car, which would continue, basically unchanged apart from styling retouches in 1969, until the end.

More was always technically possible, but BMC's product planners would never approve the work. Among the many derivatives proposed were a car with all-independent suspension by Hydrolastic units (like those used in the Minis and 1100s of the day), cars with five-speed transmissions, or alternatively with Laycock overdrives under much-modified floor pans, and more ambitious restyled bodywork.

The end, however, when it came, was abrupt, cruel, and totally unjustified by sales and marketing prospects. Like other brands in the BMC group, Austin-Healey was absorbed into the massive new British Leyland colossus in 1968, with most strategic decisions thereafter being controlled by former Leyland personnel. Within months it became clear that Leyland, and not the various BMC personalities, would shape future policy.

The chairman, Lord Stokes, previously head of Leyland, soon decided to get rid of a series of valuable BMC consultants, one of which was the Healey Motor Company, not only to save money, but because he was wrongly convinced that British Leyland could do better on its own. During 1970 he announced that the royalty agreement would shortly be terminated, and that the 'Austin-Healey' badge would be abandoned at the end of 1970. On the other hand, he had no intention of dropping the MG Midget, which was hard for Sprite enthusiasts to accept, as it could never have existed without Austin-Healey input.

And so it was. After the Austin-Healey Sprite was dropped, in order to keep Austin dealerships happy for a time an otherwise identical Austin Sprite was produced in 1971 only (just 1,022 such cars were built), while the MG Midget carried on until the end of 1979. In that decade Midgets were produced with what was known as the 'round rear-wheel arch' style from 1972 to 1974. From late 1974 the car was re-engineered, not only with massive black plastic bumpers at front and rear (the better to meet new United States crash test regulations), but with a Triumph-based 1,493cc engine and related gearbox.

The last Midget of all was built before the end of 1979, at which point all historic links with the Austin-Healey marque were lost. Though MGs were later revived in other British Leyland factories, the Austin-Healey was not.

This *Mark IV Handbook* cover shows just how little the Sprite changed, visually at least, during the 1960s, for this was the final type, produced from 1966 to 1970.

AUSTIN-HEALEY SPRITE

Specifications:
948cc (original Mark I), 1,098cc or 1,275cc (final Sprite). 43 bhp, 46 bhp, 56 bhp, 59 bhp or 65 bhp. Four-speed gearbox.

Wheelbase:
6 feet 8 inches.

Unladen weight:
1,328 pounds (original Sprite) to 1,575 pounds (final Sprite).

Top speed:
87 mph (original Sprite) to 94 mph (final Sprite).

Production:
128,337 (plus 1,022 'Austin' Sprite in 1971), and 152,627 near-identical MG Midgets.

RACING, RALLYING AND RECORD BREAKING

DONALD HEALEY had always loved motor sport, so when the chance came to use Austin-Healeys in racing, rallying and record breaking there was no hesitation. In thirty years 'pre-Austin-Healey', Donald himself had won the Monte Carlo Rally (in an Invicta in 1931), competed in all other types of motor sport, set new speed records in 'Warwick Healeys' in the 1940s, and seen those cars compete with honour at Le Mans and in the Italian Mille Miglia.

As the Austin-Healey brand developed in the 1950s, BMC was happy to see motor-sport participation used to help raise the profile of the various models, though it never spent money extravagantly on ultra-special models. Instead, careful programmes involved streamlining 100s to enable them to exceed 200 mph in speed record attempts, while long-term development ensured that the 3000s became formidable rally cars, and that Sprites could sometimes embarrass larger and more expensive rivals on the race tracks of the world.

To do this, BMC decided that Healey (at Warwick) should look after much of the motor racing, and all the record-breaking attempts, while its own official Competitions Department (which was located at the MG factory at Abingdon) should look after the rally programme. Supporting all this (gleefully and expertly guided by Eddie Maher) was the BMC Engines Branch in Coventry, with input from Downton Engineering, who had much knowledge of A-Series engine development, which could be applied to Sprites.

Happily, Healey, 'Comps' at Abingdon and the Engines Branch all co-existed happily and achieved great success. During the life of the marque, great successes were achieved as far apart as endurance record runs on the Bonneville Salt Flats in Utah, USA, on the roughest and toughest rally routes of Europe, and in prestigious motor races such as Le Mans and the Sebring 12 Hour races. Some specialised models were produced to achieve this – special streamlining for Utah, much detailed development work for the 3000s, and highly individual racing Sprites were all produced, and not least the

Opposite:
The most famous victory in the career of the 'Big Healey' came in the 1964 Spa–Sofia–Liège Marathon of 1964, which was won by Rauno Aaltonen and Tony Ambrose in BMO 93B.

lightweight 100S of the mid-1950s – but most successes were gained with cars recognisably evolved from those that were selling in their thousands.

RALLYING

In a period which retrospectively became known as the 'golden age', Austin-Healeys set new standards in rallying and made a huge marketing impact. Although Sprites were recognised as fast and plucky 'class' cars, it was the rock-solid 3000s which made most headlines.

Tommy Wisdom, a long-time Healey fan, and a successful racing driver himself, somehow squeezed into a 100S in 1955.

Gerry Burgess and Sam Croft-Pearson took tenth place overall in the 1958 Liège–Rome–Liège rally in their 'works' 100-Six, which was one of the first such cars to be prepared at Abingdon.

Pat Moss hated to rally a car carrying the number 13, and 7 plus 6 equals 13. Nevertheless, driving this phenomenal 3000, URX 727, she finished second in the 1960 French Alpine Rally, and later in the summer she also won the Liège–Rome–Liège Marathon.

Although Sprites startled the rallying world by taking third place in the very tough Liège–Sofia–Liège rally, and second in the British RAC Rally (both in 1960), it was the success of the 'Big Healeys' that made most impact. Four-cylinder 100/4 types were not used by the factory, and the 100-Six was used only until the 3000 was ready, but from 1959 that car developed

Fifty years on, Pat Moss's car is carefully and lovingly preserved, and still appears at Healey club events.

In the early 1960s the combination of 'works' Austin-Healey 3000, Pat Moss and her co-driver, Ann Wisdom, was one of the most formidable in European rallying.

All four of the 'works' 3000 team cars queuing at the bottom of the Mont Ventoux hillclimb test in the 1962 French Alpine Rally. The Morley twins, driving 57 ARX, won the event outright.

into a rugged, fast and specialised machine. That remarkable lady Pat Moss won the 96-hour marathon Liège–Rome–Liège outright in 1960 (beating all the men in the same team, and the best rival cars in Europe); Rauno Aaltonen

repeated the success in 1964, while the Morley twins won the glamorous and high-speed French Alpine event in 1961 and 1962. Healeys were fastest in several other major events, but because rally sport was infested with performance 'handicap' formulae in those days their best efforts were often buried in the results sheets. In Britain's own RAC Rally, it was the rocky tracks, and lack of traction, which defeated the 3000s, which finished a gallant second on several occasions in the 1960s but usually finished behind front-wheel-drive cars (on one occasion the winner being a Mini-Cooper S).

Even so, and until a change in regulations outlawed much of the work that had been completed (definitive 'works' cars had light-alloy body panels, alloy cylinder heads, engines with Weber carburettors, and well over 200 bhp), the 3000 was always the car by which rivals had to measure themselves, for their structures were usually rock solid, their driver strength colossal, and the team spirit unbeatable. It was not merely their performance which endeared them to Austin-Healey fanatics, but their character – for no other rival of the period sounded quite like a 3000 (the side exhaust was mostly responsible for this), nor looked quite as macho, nor bellowed, leapt and lurched from crag to crag, nor soaked up quite as much punishment.

Such cars were hand-built at Abingdon, lovingly maintained, and ruthlessly driven by superstar drivers such as Timo Makinen, Rauno Aaltonen and, of course, Pat Moss, for they were immensely strong, and in spite of their low-slung build were also able to withstand the battering

When the time came for this factory-prepared Healey 3000 to be retired from active duty, John Gott, the 'rallying policeman', bought the car and campaigned it for years in British club motor sport.

A factory team lines up prior to the start of the 1964 Spa–Sofia–Liège rally. Drivers (left to right) were Timo Makinen, Don Barrow, Rauno Aaltonen, Henry Liddon, Tony Ambrose, Paddy Hopkirk. Aaltonen won the event outright.

of rough roads that 1960s rallying doled out at the time. With the solitary exception of Porsche's high-tech 911s, no production sports car of the day was more capable, the result being that the 3000's rally reputation has persisted ever since.

RACING

For more than ten years, always from their workshops at Warwick, Healey produced a number of race cars, all based on production cars to a greater or, in some cases, lesser degree. Wherever the regulations allowed, engines were power-tuned, bodies were lightened, more efficient streamlining was evolved, and the handling was recalibrated for circuit use.

The original 100-based machines were labelled 'Special Test Cars' and competed with honour in the Italian Mille Miglia and in the prestigious Le Mans 24 Hours Race, but they always struggled against purpose-built racing sports cars, which were at once lighter, sleeker and more powerful. On the other hand, strength and race-long reliability helped, which explains a third place overall at Sebring, Florida, in 1954. Later in that year, a 'Special Test Car' averaged 74 mph in the Mille Miglia (and finished second-best non-Italian car), while in 1955 a 'works' 100S driven by Stirling Moss took sixth place in the Sebring 12 Hour Race, and George Abecassis finished eleventh in the gruelling Mille Miglia.

Unhappily, lax regulations, and the development of ultra-special racing sports cars from Healey's rivals, caused them to cut back on racing with the original big cars, though lightweight machines were campaigned with honour in the early 1960s, both in North America and in the Le Mans 24 Hour Race.

By the end of the 1950s, though, the cheeky and purposeful little Sprite came in for attention, for though it could not be expected to win races, it could, with a lot of engine development (and some attention to the streamlining of the body style, where regulations allowed), become a very effective 'class' car. The combined efforts of the Morris Engines Branch in Coventry and Downton Engineering in Wiltshire produced remarkable engines, which could sometimes propel these little cars at up to 150 mph.

Knowing that publicity was all-important, and that reliability on rough or undulating surfaces was their strong point, Healey entered Sprites at events as diverse as Sebring, Le Mans, and the Targa Florio in Sicily. Class victories in the Sebring 12 Hour Race were recorded in 1959 and 1960, and after a period of ill-fortune there were further victories in 1965, 1966, 1967,

This extremely rare colour shot, taken at the Goodwood race circuit in the early 1950s, shows off the special light green used on Healey's own Special Test Cars. NOJ 391 was one of the very first 'works' competition 100/4s.

1968 and 1969. In addition, in the Sebring Four Hour race of 1960 Stirling Moss finished second overall, which the American crowd found exhilarating. Third places in 1961 and 1962 – in both cases behind the special Italian Abarth cars – showed just how effective the little Sprites were.

Much effort went into producing Le Mans Sprites during the 1960s, especially in 1964 and 1965, when the Sprites had to compete with the very special small Triumph Spitfires. Class wins were achieved in 1960 and 1965 (that time with a different, fully streamlined, coupé body style), and in other events special cars raced by teams such as the Dick Jacobs team performed with real honour.

That cars developed from such mundane origins should become effective and successful race cars might have been surprising, but if their brand name included the magical name of 'Healey' it was not.

From 1962, factory-built race and rally Healey 3000s were fitted with aluminium cylinder heads and three twin-choke Weber carburettors, producing more than 210 bhp.

LONG-DISTANCE RECORDS

Right from the start, Donald Healey and his colleagues gained BMC approval to chase, beat and set new high-speed endurance records with the 100/4 and its successors. In 1953 a machine of standard appearance – one of the original Special Test Cars – was sent to the Bonneville Salt Flats to attack a number of American national records, which were achieved most successfully. Not only did this car reach 142.64 mph in a straight line, but it kept going at 123 mph for twelve hours, and a standard car kept going, on a 10 mile circular salt-surfaced track, for more than 5,000 km, at 103.94 mph. A year later, Healey (with help and advice from BMC's aerodynamic specialists) produced a long-nose/long-tail streamliner with a supercharged 2.6-litre engine, which achieved more than 190 mph over short distances. Meanwhile a standard-looking 'endurance' car went out on the circular track and circled for no less than twenty-four hours, setting new marks at 132.33 mph.

Finally, in 1956, the visually modified streamliner went back to Bonneville with a supercharged 292 bhp version of the new six-cylinder

Healey and BMC produced this startlingly reshaped version of the BN1, complete with a supercharged engine, to attack American speed records at the Bonneville Salt Flats in 1954.

Although it was
never developed
for circuit racing,
Donald Healey
demonstrated the
Bonneville record
car at Silverstone
in May 1955.

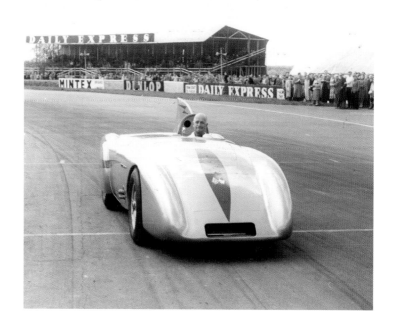

Two special cars,
for two different
record attempts
on the Bonneville
Salt Flats in 1956.
Donald Healey
and two colleagues
pose behind the
long-nose/long-tail
version of the
prototype 100-Six,
while behind it is
the much-modified
supercharged
'streamliner',
which achieved
more than
200 mph.

engine, with the hope of exceeding 200 mph. Although it suffered engine trouble on the run itself, 203 mph was achieved. In the meantime, a modified 100-Six prototype (with longer nose and tail sections) ran for more than six hours, at speeds up to 153.50 mph.

This was the end of a very successful four-year programme, which proved its worth, both in the record books, and to North America's 'showroom traffic', who were impressed by what they saw.

The Sprite was never involved in record breaking, with one rather artificial exception. This was in 1959, when BMC took one of its ageing MG record cars (which had started life as EX 179), gave it a supercharged Sprite 948cc engine, which developed 98 bhp in 'one hour' form, or up to 86 bhp for longer-duration attempts, and set it to tackle endurance marks at Bonneville. EX 219, as the new 'Austin-Healey' was called, duly ran and ran and ran – clocking 146.95 mph for one hour, and no less than 138.75 mph for an all-day twelve-hour stint.

Although EX 219 survived to become a much-respected display car, the other record cars did not. Though amply strong and suitable for their task at the time, they all suffered from severe salt blast in their high-speed runs, corroded badly and were eventually cut up and given a decent burial. Legend has it that there is ground close to the old factory at Warwick which contains those remains.

The Austin-Healey race car that never was: the Healey SR was built at Warwick and raced at Le Mans with a Coventry-Climax V8 engine. (This is a charming modern replica of the original 1970 model, seen at Goodwood.)

JENSEN-HEALEY AND REPLICAS

A LTHOUGH cast adrift by British Leyland in 1970, Donald Healey never gave up hope of reviving a line of sports cars which carried his name. After forging an alliance with Jensen of West Bromwich, which had produced almost all the body/chassis units for the larger Austin-Healeys, he joined the board, became chairman for a time and inspired the birth of the Jensen-Healey.

Created with the intention of making a similar car to the earlier generation, and to appeal to North American buyers, the Jensen-Healey of 1972 was a compact two-seater sports car, this time with a unit-construction body/chassis unit. Though powered by a 2-litre sixteen-valve

Lotus twin-cam engine, which produced 144 bhp, and neat in its style, with a top speed of nearly 120 mph, it was not backed by a big dealer network and struggled to survive. Although it was later joined by a 'sporting estate' version called Jensen GT (the Healey name having been dropped), the project died away when Jensen struck financial trouble in 1976.

Although 10,504 Jensen-Healeys (and 507 Jensen GTs) were produced, and the future looked bright, the company could not gain any financial support in what were inflationary times from a government that favoured the pie-in-the-sky claims of DeLorean instead, and this car was never revived. It was the last serious sports-car project with which Donald Healey was connected.

In later years, replicas (perhaps better referred to as lookalikes) of both the 'Frog-eye' Sprite and the 3000 were developed and found a limited market, but none of these cars had the backing of the Healey family and should never be confused with the originals. The Frog Eye, which was devised by an Isle of Wight entrepreneur, was a comprehensively re-engineered and updated pastiche of the original (complete with the startling headlamp position) and attracted the qualified approval of Geoffrey Healey. Re-creations of the larger 3000, under various names, were not as successful and, complete with glass-fibre bodies, extended wheel arches and a variety

For the Jensen-Healey project, Healey adopted the new sixteen-valve twin-cam Lotus engine, which was technically more advanced than anything ever fitted to Austin-Healey models.

of non-original engines, did not gain his favour. It was a measure of the love of originality by true Austin-Healey enthusiasts that none of these cars was swept into the wider movement.

In the 1990s and 2000s several attempts were made to revive the brand – some with the support of the Healey family (which retained 'branding' rights) and some not – but none came to fruition. BMW (which owned the Rover Group for six traumatic years between 1994 and 2000) was reputed to be looking at a revival using BMW components, but nothing came of this.

In the 2000s one 'company doctor' and entrepreneur bought up the rights of the discontinued (German) Smart Roadster Coupé, to turn it into a latter-day Sprite, while a British Austin-Healey parts manufacturer proposed to build a new 3-litre engined sports car (this project had the backing of the Healeys), but, although both stated that they would build 'Austin-Healey' cars in new factories in South Wales, nothing ever followed the original announcements.

The enduring popularity of the Austin-Healey is clear in this modern reproduction HMC 3000.

The famous Austin-Healey brand, therefore, has a clearly defined life span – from 1952, when the very first Healey 100 became the Austin-Healey 100, to 1970, when the very last Austin-Healey Sprite was built at Abingdon. The love of these cars continues unabated, with the size and vibrant activities of the many one-make clubs proving that true enthusiasms never die.

FURTHER READING

Anderson, Gary, and Moment, Roger. *Austin-Healey 100/100-Six/3000 Restoration Guide*. Motorbooks, 2000.
Clausager, Anders Ditlev. *Original Austin-Healey*. Bay View Books, 1990.
Clausager, Anders Ditlev. *Sprites and Midgets*. Crowood Press, 1991.
Clausager, Anders Ditlev. *Original Sprite and Midget*. Bay View Books, 1994.
Edwards, Jonathan. *Sprite and Midget*. Crowood Press, 2002.
Healey, Geoffrey. *The Healey Story*. Haynes Publishing, 1996.
Piggott, Bill. *Haynes Great Cars: Austin-Healey*. Haynes Publishing, 2002.
Piggott, Bill. *Austin-Healey 100 in Detail*. Herridge & Sons, 2005.
Robson, Graham. *Austin-Healey 100 and 3000 Series*. Crowood Press, 2001.

CLUBS

All round the world, there are dozens of clubs which look after the interests and preservation of the Austin-Healey marque. The author recommends the use of an Internet search engine to locate them. The principal British clubs are:

The Austin-Healey Club: Colleen Holmes, 4 Saxby Street, Leicester LE2 0ND. Website: www.austin-healey-club.com
Healey Drivers Club: Malcolm Lorraine, Little Burwood, Red Lane, Bugle, St Austell, Cornwall PL26 8QP. Website: www.healeydriversclub.co.uk
The Midget and Sprite Club: Nigel Williams, 15 Foxcote, Kingswood, Bristol BS15 2TX. Website: www.mgcars.org.uk

PLACES TO VISIT

Museum displays may be altered and readers are advised to check before travelling that the relevant vehicles are on show and to ascertain the opening times. An up-to-date listing of all road transport museums in the United Kingdom can be found on www.motormuseums.com

Haynes International Motor Museum, Sparkford, Yeovil, Somerset BA22 7LH. Telephone: 01963 440804. Website: www.haynesmotormuseum.co.uk
Heritage Motor Centre, Banbury Road, Gaydon, Warwickshire CV35 0BJ. Telephone: 01926 641188. Website: www.heritage-motor-centre.co.uk
National Motor Museum, John Montagu Building, Beaulieu, Brockenhurst, Hampshire SO42 7ZN. Telephone: 01590 612345. Website: www.beaulieu.co.uk

INDEX

Page numbers in italics refer to illustrations